BORROWED ROOMS

borrowed rooms

Barbara Pelman

RONSDALE PRESS

BORROWED ROOMS
Copyright © 2008 Barbara Pelman

RONSDALE PRESS
3350 West 21st Avenue
Vancouver, B.C., Canada V6S 1G7
www.ronsdalepress.com

Typesetting: Julie Cochrane, in New Baskerville 11 pt on 13.5
Cover Design: Julie Cochrane
Cover Photo: Julie Cochrane
Author Photo: Sandy McElroy, 2008
Paper: Ancient Forest Friendly Silva — 100% post-consumer waste, totally
    chlorine-free and acid-free

Ronsdale Press wishes to thank the following for their support of its publishing program: the Canada Council for the Arts, the Government of Canada through the Book Publishing Industry Development Program (BPIDP), and the Province of British Columbia through the Book Publishing Tax Credit Program and the British Columbia Arts Council.

Library and Archives Canada Cataloguing in Publication

Pelman, Barbara
   Borrowed rooms / Barbara Pelman.

Poems.
ISBN 978-1-55380-061-3

   I. Title.

PS8631.E4685B67 2008   C811'.6   C2008-904785-0

At Ronsdale Press we are committed to protecting the environment. To this end we are working with Markets Initiative (www.oldgrowthfree.com) and printers to phase out our use of paper produced from ancient forests. This book is one step towards that goal.

Printed in Canada by Marquis Book Printing, Quebec, Canada

to my mother
and my daughter
with love

and to my father,
Solomon (Pucky) Pelman
(1915–2006) z'l

CONTENTS

Back to the Ordinary

—

Between Affection and Flight

—

In Everything That Sings

—

Directions of the Heart

—

ACKNOWLEDGEMENTS

Many thanks to my editor, Susan Stenson, for her incisions and concisions, and her warm heart. Thanks also to Patrick Lane, whose Glenairley retreats keep the soul alive and the mind tough; and to Wendy Morton, poetry promoter extraordinaire. Most especially, to my writing group, the Waywords, who helped inspire and mend these poems, button up their little coats and send them out the door. And thanks to Ronald Hatch of Ronsdale Press for welcoming the poems in.

Some of these poems have appeared in *The Antigonish Review, Descant, Contemporary Verse 2, Quills Magazine, Fiddlehead* and in the *Leaf Press Chapbooks: The Glenairley series.* Three of the poems have appeared as the Monday Poem on the Leaf Press website.

"In the Bird Sanctuary" won second prize in the Quills Poetry Contest 2007, "Simka" was a finalist in the Rona Murray Poetry Contest 2007, and "Magnolia" won honourable mention in the December Press Contest 2008.

—

In "Shutting Down," the phrase *innocence without heartbreak* is taken from the short story "A Bolt of White Cloth" by Leon Rooke.

Baba Yaga is the mythical figure of Russian fairy tales: powerful and mysterious. She lives in a hut which rests on chicken legs, in the deep forest. This particular Baba Yaga owes much to the one in "Women Who Run with the Wolves" by Clarissa Pinkola Estes.

The name *Sadie* is from the song "Sadie Sadie Married Lady" in the film "Funny Girl."

In "Adam's Dilemma," Elohim is the name of God used in the first Creation story; *re'ut, ditzah, chevda, gilah,* and *ahavah* are names of the variations of marital joy mentioned in the Jewish marriage ceremony. *Selah*, translated in English as "rib" referring to the creation of Eve, actually means "side" or "wall" in Hebrew.

Yevorechecha mentioned in the poems about my father, is the blessing after the *Amidah* prayer in the Shabbat service. It is translated in English as: *May the Lord bless you and keep you.*

"Four Directions of the Heart" borrows a line from Patrick Lane's poem: "Dominion Day Dance": *[it] has entered him like a cage enters an animal.*

"Nothing to Be Owned" is based on Rabbi Harry Brechner's interpretation of the first chapter of the fourth book of the Bible, Numbers — in Hebrew, *Ba'Midbar,* "In the Desert." The text of *Ba'Midbar* suggests that in order to receive Torah, or spiritual awareness, one must be *hegveyr*, like the desert itself — open and vulnerable and ownerless.

Back to
the Ordinary

Any place I hang my hat is home

— JOHNNY MERCER

Back to the Ordinary

That in between time
when your clothes still smell of the beach
you walked along that morning, but the stone
in your pocket has faded from its bright
pinks and purples; on your hands
is a faint whiff of seaweed, and there is sand
between your toes, the trace of surf
still sounding in your ears. The ordinary world
has not yet clutched you, your books seem
unfamiliar, something someone else
might have chosen; the couch holds the ghost
of someone you might have known. Perhaps this
is just another hotel room, another place to set
a hat or a suitcase; nothing really yours, not
the trees in the yard or the dahlias
you planted in the garden; not the photos
on the fridge or the paintings on the wall;
no more than the long sand
where you shivered at its watery edges,
the sea anemones drying between the rocks.

A Room Full of Light

after Yeats' "Lake Isle of Innisfree"

I will burn these papers, and head to a quiet shore
where I will rent a villa, fill a room full of light,
shells on the window sill; outside, feathers of tamarisk,
and I will be alone, and like it.

Nothing entangled, the threads of thought long and shining
so quiet I can hear the yellow warbler weave twigs for a nest
in the morning's shimmer, and later, noon's hot halo
and evening full of wings and wind.

I could catch a plane, quickly, while the restless heart is bold,
while I can still hear the warbler, the sound of leaves
in the breeze. But I am at my desk, the rustle is only of paper
that freezes the deep heart, seizes the mind's core.

Hawthorn

Hawthorn after rain:
wind and wet and white, blossoms
again into green

Hawthorn in the back garden:
a nest for sparrows,
made of berry and blossom.

After the winter storms, one
flicker hunts insects
at the edge of the patio.

Rain on a Sunday morning:
I watch the clouds across the water
gather, glower, and drop —

wind follows. *Watch for wind*
he always said: a change in weather —
perhaps a change in me.

And more to come, these oasis days —
not the Garden, but not desert either.
The rain falls,

wet and song-filled,
the sparrow's cadenza
descants above the traffic,

and the crows bully the juncos.
This summer I'll build
a Zen garden,

white with silence, on the patio,
one yellow rose bush
in the centre —

blossoms in the mind, a hint
of fragrance,
wind from new directions

again, sails tight,
the boat angled and racing,
feet bare, pay out the lines

into taut measures, wind against flashing water,
turn
and turn again —

green hills in the distance, gulls calling
a lost name: and the rose bush
among white stones.

Note on the form:
"Hawthorn" is an extended haiku. Each word from the original
haiku begins a stanza. Each stanza is in itself a haiku, containing
approximately seventeen syllables. The form was suggested in
conversation with David Kaetz, a musician.

Talisman for Summer

in the style of a terza rima

Toes curled at the edge of the deck,
warm planks of fir and maple, the sun
above the mast, sails full — I check

the lines, coil them in neat spirals, each one
in its separate place, as I've been taught.
First mate's duty is never done

he reminds me, and I keep the sails taut,
the tiller straight. The wind is strong,
the ship leans into the water, light caught

in the shimmer of hull and wave, a long
line of summer: bare legs and arms,
happy rags of shirt and shorts, the song

of quiet evenings — the winter storm
of stress and deadline gone, forgotten
for a little while, a little moment worn

like a talisman: white sails in a blue breeze.

The Perfect Hotel

It must have a bathtub,
with faucets in the middle, so lovers
can lie back, toes touching, bubbles
from a small bottle scenting the heat.
Like the room above Friday Harbour,
overlooking sloops and schooners,
the morning ferry from Anacortes.

It must have room service,
a red rose in a glass vase, pewter
tea pot, basket of croissants
and the morning paper: the *Times*.
Good coffee in crisp white mugs. A window
overlooking the Thames, lighting
the bed with neon and shadow.

It must have the sound of morning:
a robin pecking the grass, fox sparrow
in the cedar, rocks tumbling in the creek
at the edge of the garden. A high bed
overlooking the willows and aspens,
the greens and grays of early spring
in the Kootenay Valley.

It must have the sound of the sea:
waves against rock, the rhythm of tide,
arbutus branches bent to the shape of wind
and the stutter of shoreline. A path
winding down to water, tidal pools
pocked with rain, the small inhabitants
busy in their drowned city.

It must have a fireplace, with wood
ready, and paper, and kindling, and good air.
Smell of cedar in the grate, sound of yellow
fingers snapping. The slow glimmer of embers,
red against the blackened logs.
It must have books, no TV or radio, a view
to elsewhere. Time is a distant thing
that others wear on their wrist, and is measured
by the light in the morning, the darkening sky.

It is the space between the waves, the sudden
flight of an eagle across the window. It is the slow
unfolding of bud, the rain shining the bones
of trees on the beach, it is the sea
drifting into sky, a no point in the centre
where you know you have been and are no longer.

Sestina for Pousada Infante, Sagres

January. Our house on the water
almost built, our daughter at college, and we,
married a dozen years, take a couple of weeks
to rest, return to a country we had loved
together. Our pockets thin:
only credit cards and a few

escudos. A few
hours ago we landed in Lisbon, headed for water
at the edge of land, a thin
peninsula jutting into the Atlantic, where we
settled into the New Year. A night of love
perhaps, then a week

to wander Portugal. Just a week
out of deadlines and papers and meetings, so few
nights together, hard to find love
in between the hellos and goodbyes, too much water
under the bridge — blood sometimes, we
think, a long stretch that thins

all expectations, our dreams thinning
out. Yet there will be a house: in a few weeks
a doorway, rooms, a place where we
can relax at the end of days, so few
together. We will listen to the water
pound under our window, consider love.

And shouldn't I be happy? Wasn't this love?
A room at the edge of the world, a thin
wedge between the weighted days, slow water
in the tub where we soak away the heavy weeks
in a space that holds so few
words. How little I knew where we

were heading. We walk the cliffs of Sagres, we
buy carpets for our tiled floors, love
the bold colours, pay with credit, what's a few
more dollars of debt? A thin
coating of fear to cover the mortgage, more weeks
than I can count to pay and pay. But there is the water

in front of us, water at our doorstep, and couldn't we
make a thin stretch of happiness in the few days to come,
and wasn't this weak, tentative thing, love?

Ghost

I could be the ghost of my own life returning
to the places I lived best.
— Linda Gregg

On the bureau, a bowl — red, glazed. In it,
his unpocketed quarters and dimes, boarding passes,
old parking stubs. A painting on the dark wall:
two Adirondack chairs facing out to the water,
wooden slats of the wharf still gleaming with new planks,
and a man, glass in hand, his bald head gleaming also.
A small vase on the windowsill, wildflowers from the meadow:
lupin and Queen Anne's lace, a sprig of salal,
false Solomon's seal. It is a small room,
almost all bed, a white duvet,
two pillows against the iron headboard,
new sheets, a pale yellow, bought recently
to replace the moldy ones left in the cabin
during hard winters and long absence, and against the wall
the bureau with its many drawers. Has he emptied these?
Has he taken out her bright shirts, the ones they bought
in Thailand, the Chinese ones he brought back from his trips —
with letters that might have spelled "luck" or "misfortune"
if she only knew.

Sestina to Landfall

Landfall, forty-five feet
of wood and grace, our classic ketch
and summer home. Every weekend
he'd paint and putter, caulk the decks
while I cleaned the galley, stored
summer shirts and shorts, coiled lines.

In July we toss off the deadlines
and schedules, let our feet
breathe free of shoes, open up stored
conversations, haul the four-sailed ketch
into a blue sky, lie on warm decks
letting weeks stretch out from weekends.

And the slow days end
in an anchored bay, a long line
of arm and leg, relaxed on the deck.
Morning coffee in the cockpit, our feet
touching. *Did you catch
any fish?* I ask, and we check our dwindling store

of supplies. *What's for dinner? Is there a store
nearby?* Feasts of salmon, crab, fresh bread, a weekend
of wind and water and wine, the ketch
smooth in the summer breeze. All lines
taut, a belly of sail, each tack a feat
of skill and terror, *Landfall's* deck

angled in a following sea, the captain decked
in Tilley hat and ragged shorts. Suits and ties stored
in a land-locked closet. Bare feet
and odd tan lines, and at day's end,
another safe harbour. We tie the lines
around each other. And now the ketch

and the marriage are up for sale. Never to catch
another breeze, haul another sheet, deck
ourselves in different attitudes. All lines
coiled and dusty. Time to store
the dreams in canvas bags, spend weekends
alone in the garden, on the beaches, feet

still bare, lines of netting tied to the deck
of the patio for sweet pea to climb. Just a white ketch,
another ending of another story, a feat of forgetting.

Small Hotels

They hide in back roads along hedgerows
of hawthorn, small birds in the tangled
branches. A restored manor on a cobbled alley,
where hooves and heels click an echo
through narrow streets. A smudged address
found by word of mouth. Brick and ivy,
water lilies, orchestra of frog and cricket
by a still lake, or beside a creek —
morning noise of current against pebble.

Small hotels: for the young ones fresh
with desire; the abandoned ones who still
clutch maps to places that no longer
exist; the broken ones who have almost lost
the need to dream; all those who limp,
who dance, who wander in the rain,
who sit by windows, those who wait.

Shutting Down

Saudade

Ridiculous even to contemplate:
that rising sense of joy, a bud
at the centre of the heart, lovers
skating parallel all their lives; *innocence*
without heartbreak, Eden built out of
ruined abbeys, or never lost. Everyone
finding their someones just in time.
Imagine a rose, yellow petals shadowed
with pink, scent of tea, and the buds
among the leaves. No aphids or
invisible worms. Imagine a pine table,
the rose in a glass vase, two place settings,
sterling silver, crystal, the wine
heavy like two mouths.

Once

In Portugal we listened to fado music
in cobbled alleyways. Honeysuckle
climbed out of tiny pots, curled around doorways.
The *pousada* windows framed almond blossom,
their heavy scent among the pillows
where we lay in the afternoons.
I should be happy, I thought,
looking out over the straight lines of olive trees,
the sun crisscrossing silver leaves,
birds somewhere.

Building the house
All that salal

Opening
The mouths
of anemones:
petals
or tentacles

Before it all began
I told him about my friends: how they took each other to
    dinner
once a month, talked about their marriage, what was
    happening between them:
"I'd never do that," he said.

They sit on the patio
The woodpecker beats a staccato
on the balsam, the wind
rattles the arbutus leaves.
"What are you thinking?" I ask.
"Nothing. I'm just listening."

Monday morning, early winter
Headlights cut the darkness,
ignition cuts the silence

ferry line-up at 6 a.m.

sunrise over the islands
orange and lavender

The house sold

I missed the ferry by two minutes
that would have closed my life
on the island. Back to the house,
key still in hand, I run the bath,
lie in the tub watching the trees
scratch the window. A few more hours,
merely a delay. The rooms already still.

Swans

Seventeen, white against the gray water:
the winter light slanting down the harbour
I stand on the wharf, counting.

Openings again

Perhaps there is always
a second chance. Pick up the dice,
roll them along the green baize,
the open palm
where a finger traces
lines and whorls,
a kiss like grace
hesitant and unexpected.

Things

She took everything from that house
except the few things she left him:
his mother's Moorcroft vases, the new sofa,
a few perfect hand-turned wood bowls,
the boat key. She packed up the paintings,
the pottery bowls and plates, the stone turtle.
On the mantel of the new house
she placed the African sculpture
called *Woman, Thinking*. Beside it,
the Balinese dancer. The wooden spoons
from Kaslo hung from hooks in the kitchen.
She would have things. They would have the power
to hurt her, but they were beautiful.

All You Need

A small house.
the sound of water —
the sea, a running river:
this is all you need.

Is this all?
one porcelain plate,
one pillow on the bed,
myself to myself in the night?

And the night,
its long hours of dreams
the half remembered places
where I have been and never been.

Where have I been
that I arrive here?
the wide bed,
the long dreams.

and the longing, the dreaming:
is it better to open the door,
dance out on a limb
wavering and stretching?

Wavering, like morning thoughts
looking out over water:
this is all you need.
This is what I have.

Dirge

after Lorca

You weave farewells out of long sighs.
Inside my head, the fingers of clouds
write a slow fugue of last words.

It is an illusion: a compassionate god.
Love is written on a stone, then tossed away.
The horizon is flat and you disappear.

The road ahead is brown and brittle.
The autumn oak clutches its leaves
like an ancient purse, full of pebbles.

I long for your quick laugh, your youth,
the days of red pomegranates, and the willow
bending her green hair into the water.

The horizon is flat and the road is long.
Your words weave a stillness in the thick air.

The Divorce Papers Finally Come Through

When the country you live in isn't yours
anymore, and the lease runs out
for the rented rooms, bare now:
the suitcases sit outside the door.

When the passport has expired, the stamps
to places you barely remember fade;
when the photo of you is a stranger's face,
the eyes searching for a landscape you have lost

or perhaps never had, seen from a tour bus
on a busy street; or cobbled alleys
of another time, the sound of horses,
the scrape of carriage wheels: all grace and glamour

or so you thought — pictures in a dusty book
no longer useful, no longer valid or true.

The Angel of Backyards

likes the perspective of rearview mirrors,
sits backwards in buses and subways
checks behind her when she walks
down back alleys —

is left-handed, has lost
the front door key, sits on the porch
contemplating last spring's garden.
She is a connoisseur of weeds

knows the yellow sharpness of broom,
the white exuberance of yarrow,
counts dandelions and buttercups
among her friends.

The angel of backyards
steals through closed doors, plants
an oblique desire in the darkest
of corners, catches you unaware

while cooking soup, planting petunias,
preparing careful budgets; digs up
buried bones, turns the compost
and there it is again — all that you thought
you lost, all you wish to lose.

Gauze

Sometimes it happens: you lose everything
and wake in the strange room of what you want.
— Tim Lilburn

Everything you thought was yours: the house
by the water, built carefully from plans you made;
summers sailing in the Gulf Islands, moored
in a bay, the night sky over the cockpit;
someone by your side, to come home to,
until death do us part, or so
you believed. A family. You thought
you had it all, had arrived at the place
your mother told you was good; *sometimes*
it happens: you lose everything.

Not suddenly, though the final tear
feels like that. The fabric has been worn thin
but it was only gauze to begin with. You wander
through your days, the scenery off-kilter
and unfamiliar. You try your hand at the new
and the exotic: art classes, flute lessons,
belly dancing, pilates. The wrecked heart
repairs itself, though you are not aware of it.
You sleep. You work. And one day you *wake*
in the strange room of what you want.

Room at the Table

The morning sun draws long shadows on the patio,
olive trees in the orchard scent the wind;
sea and a garden, and three small rooms.

I had packed everything in boxes,
sold the house in the city —
here, beside the olive groves I could see
what there is to see.

I place my books on the windowsill,
the sea visible if I shift my chair.
Wisteria frames the window.

Three old men and a woman, faces to the sun,
under the bougainvillea edging the patio next door.
They sit, eyes closed, cheeks etched in wrinkles,
smile and say nothing.

I will walk to the beach, lay out a towel
and books, feel the sting of salt, shiver
and awaken: another shell tossed onto the shore

neither homeless nor abandoned, shining
as the sun catches an edge. Small boats
painted blue, yellow, red, set out to sea
as the current shifts —

I will learn the names
of every flower and tree on the island.
Soon even I will have a name in this place.

The waiter at the café will greet me, and I will reply
Kalhemera and order another espresso.
I'll buy bread and cheese, choose a wine —
perhaps invite someone to dinner.

The Mars Hotel: 1950

based on a photograph of two
elderly women and a neon sign

It was a rainy day, just like this,
she says. That hotel,
the Mars. He took me there,
and we watched the rain
glaze the windows all day.
I was too scared, I tell you.
The way the desk clerk looked at me,
like he could see right down
to my underwear. He gave the key
as if it were a red-hot invitation
to Hell. And then,
that bed. Seemed huge,
the thin chenille bedspread
a faded yellow. It was a long
time ago, but I remember
his voice, a kind of scratchy
velvet. And his hands, long
fingers like a piano player.
He wanted to play me, he laughed,
but I couldn't move. Big words
had got me there. Sure, I had said,
let's get this virginity thing
over with. Then that bed.

His words were kind, but I knew
he was angry. Spent all that money
on a hotel room, and there I was,
huddled on the easy chair, knuckles
white. Maybe he should've
just done it. Maybe it would have been
better, break through the silk walls,
untie the knots in my head.

I never saw him again. Don't blame him.
We should've been floating out of that hotel
red-cheeked and glowing like the neon
sign: Mars, the red planet, passion boiling
out of every rock.

That was a long time ago. I guess
he's married, somebody who knows
her mind, gives him what he wants
and she wants it too. Never mind.
Want some tea? There's a place
down the road. We can stop there.
My feet are killing me.

Chagall's Red Tree

You wake up one day and nothing is the same.
The tree is on fire, the branches —
scripture inside the flames.
Fox, you say, but the eyes
looking out at you from the tree
ignore you. Moon, you say, sky,
but what is this yellow crescent,
this smudge of candle and shadow?
Nothing seems what it is:
these cleft feet,
this green body beside you.
Somewhere, the sound
of violins, a hand on your belly,
the scent of leaves, the heat.
The city where you once lived
is dark, the gates closed. How
can you trust this horned creature,
his moon eyes? Even the angel
trumpeting all is well sounds silly
and false. Who can blame you
for hiding behind a necklace of stars?

Icarus' Sister

They left me in the labyrinth.
You'll be safe here, they said,
nothing but the long corridors
and the walls. Frankly, I don't think
they thought much about me. *Never look
back* was my father's motto.

While they built the frame,
measured and hammered,
I collected feathers. Stood on the rooftop
coaxed birds to my welcoming hands,
plucked them as they flew by. The long
primaries from the albatross, the grey
fingers of osprey, the shadow of storm petrel
as it passed the stone towers. Once
a frigate bird soared overhead, its huge
wings like a dark thought. I lengthened
my arm, caught a tail feather, gave it
to Icarus. Slowly the contraption
from my father's mind became wings.

All those days
they searched for a way out,
watched the tern, the kite,
the various gulls — their soar,
their glide, their hover. All those days
I walked through the maze,
sure of my direction, knowing
the small crevice in the deepest
wall, knowing how to turn my body
into spider and mouse. While they
hammered and glued, I walked the hills,
the wide meadows of Mykonos.
I didn't tell them, of course.

When they leave, when they head
for the light, their grand adventure,
their hero story, the splash
that was heard the world over,

I will walk to Heraclion,
pluck olives from the tree,
collect grapes from the neighbour's
arbor, sit on the hillside:
watch my brother fall.

Mother and Daughter to Thailand

The suitcase sits beside the bed, wide mouth
gaping, assessing each skirt and shirt
I offer. The list grows longer, as I gather
worries from every corner of the universe. What if
we lose each other in Bangkok? What if
I can't find my way to the hotel? What if the sex trade grabs her,
if drug dealers or traffic accidents get us? What if
we fight? What if
we run out of money, time, patience?
Should I buy a cellphone or palm pilot,
a digital camera, more currency,
a tank top, maps, first-aid kit, antibiotics, salt tablets,
water distiller, jet lag tablets, insect repellent, —
better get anxiety repellent, she tells me.
The guidebooks overwhelm with options:
budget, mid-range, high-end hotels. Easy, moderate
grueling tours. Safe, middle of the road, terrifying
adventures. Only the weather
offers no choice: hot and steamy
from saffron dawn to indigo dusk,
then dark and steamy, insect-nibbled night.

First time off the cliff of the continent, free fall
across a thousand years, gold-laced temples,
birds with names like oil palettes: red rumped
green woodpecker, white-crested laughingthrush,
coppersmith barbet; animals familiar only
in children's books: elephant and rhino,
macaque and leopard. Floating markets,
chilies a red gash across the eye, fabric
a choreography of colour, and everywhere
the tropical sun.

I will return changed, new blessings
on my tongue, new shapes
to form into words, a daughter
newly known.

Bodies

At Thong Ta Pan Resort, the Little Beach,
a woman sits at water's edge
reading a book, wears a hat
and her bikini bottom —
breasts small, nipples pink
like morning flowers.
Farther down the sand,
another woman reaches up
to kiss her lover, whose hands hover
in mid-air, longing to touch
her round tanned breasts.
Near where I sit,
a woman poses in a lime-green thong:
her breasts like full wineskins
brown and leathered. Her son
records her on video for the family
back in Italy.

I take off my long-sleeved shirt,
baggy trousers, strip down to one piece
swimsuit, once pointed breasts
flattened under red lycra:
cover it all again with a red
tie-dye sarong.

A body that once cartwheeled across tidal sands,
jetéd in circles around a bare stage,
whose knees once pistoned into pirouettes;
breasts now point downward and outwards
showing a cleavage of bare ribs — its fine points
hidden under a burka of cellulite and wrinkles.
I am told that Brazilian women wear their bodies
with pride, wrinkle and fold and tuck and belly.
I wear mine like a shapeless coat that needs
mending, tuckered and out of style.

From This Distance

It begins with a key in your pocket,
your suitcase emptied into drawers and closets —
a place you can return to, with pillows
and restless dreams. You open the wooden shutters
to almond blossoms, snow in the spring leaves.
The olive trees line up in rows,
their silver undersides catch the wind like sparks.
A man walks in twilight down a cobbled road,
his sheep follow him from their day in the hills.
From this distance the pieces of your broken world
fall differently, you can see the bright edges,
feel the wind sculpt the rocks into a shape
that could be a haven, an oasis,
that you might, for a little while, call home.

Between Affection and Flight

—

For nothing can be sole or whole
that has not been rent.

— W.B. YEATS, "CRAZY JANE TALKS
WITH THE BISHOP"

Winter Sketches

December

The rain has stopped and the sky,
though gray, is streaked with light.
One tall pine, a thin
calligraphy, sways in a morning wind.

The different greens: moss
on rock, the matte green of lawn,
deeper green of the tall fir
in the neighbour's yard. And the oak
still clutching its brown fingers
around an agitated leaf.

January

When the snow stops, the sky
is a pale dusty grey
like the morning coat
of an aristocrat, the snow
a starched collar, immaculate cuffs,
and the tree's bark is polished
like a patent pump.

Three branches curve with a white
shadow, the wooden fence
is capped with white, snow drops
in wet clumps, covering a waiting
green.

February

A blinding white, this foot of snow
and so still, except when a branch
suddenly loosens its burden of heavy
down, and then a spray of white and dull green,
then stillness again. A light snow still falling,
drifting rather, and a washed pewter sky.

The cedar leans its fat white fingers
over the fence, the summer umbrella
I forgot to take in, broken by the wind,
is now a white boat
filled with winter, floating on a white sea.

February still

Clear and cold. Even the first bird
this winter morning is white:
a small gull, in from the strait,
surprised to find a white river below her
beside the still grey sea.
Yesterday's footprints have frozen
into deep valleys.

March

Green begins to return,
uncovered by melting snow.
It was always there,
of course. White patches
like a child's finger painting.
Tree branches bob in green,
the pin oak clutches its withered leaves.
Mountains float above fog,
edged in white, and a bird
slides past my eye, too quick
for my morning pen.

Grounded and Pensive

In the dim unwritten folklore of the heart
they are the soft grey sisters
　　　　　　— Don McKay, "Mourning Doves"

Yesterday, on the fence railing
a hawk, perhaps stalking the grey squirrels
bold as exclamation marks
claiming my garden.
He is a stranger here, in a city landscape,
townhouses and condos
that once were his fields and meadows.
His keen yellow eyes search for grass
where small mice might be hiding.
In the dim unwritten folklore of the heart

he is the lost power, the hunter
Orion, traffic lights instead of stars.
He grinds his beak on the soft wood,
flexes claws, wings cribbed by tree and bush,
his sky-blue world too brown, too close.
What is a hunter to do, grounded
and pensive? What worlds to challenge
his sharp eye, his penchant
for the throat? Only an empty sky, clouds:
the soft grey sisters.

Considering Falling in Love after Sixty

He'll be old, probably bald,
skin tags at his neck — his grandchildren
will be the age of my students, maybe
are my students. He'll have bad habits
he won't want to break, old friends
who've known him longer than I have life
yet to live.

          Why share my bed?
His feet will be cold. He'll pull the covers off
at midnight, breathe in fortissimo, fling
his arm over my back at dawn. He may be fond
of old plaid bathrobes, leave beard bits
in the sink, the toilet seat up.

I'd have to learn not to lick my fingers
or the knife, bake something more original
than my mother's banana muffins.
I'd have to consider cooking at all,
meals at definite hours, his diet of broccoli,
or worse, parsnip casserole.

I'd have to find a way to claim
the spaces necessary for breath, learn
how to claim any space at all. Remember
not to suffocate from smiling, learn again
the word no is not goodbye.

I'd have to learn to pick up the pieces
from a puzzle, know its blank spaces,
the shapes, the satisfying fit
when the colours match, and the round bulge
slides into the round bowl, and the image
arises, the whole from the broken.

Argument

Sadie:

All my life I've been told:
marriage is the natural state of man.
A challenge, sure, but worth it.
Till death do us part: learn the dance,
lead and follow, sidestep and bend;
two is better than one.

Baba Yaga:

Lead and follow: who leads?
The shadow of a man is very long.

Sadie:

Without a man you're nothing.
Nobody notices you. You're on the shelf,
stale dated.

Baba Yaga:

Put books and vases on the shelf.
Hold nothing in your arms.

Sadie:

The bed is so wide, my body invisible.
Who will see me, under these layers:
clothes, wrinkles, folds.

Baba Yaga:

Beds are for sleeping. Bodies are for dancing.

Sadie:

We are made to be two: yin and yang,
yolk and egg, male and female are one.

Baba Yaga:

God is One.

Sadie:

Saturday nights are long. The phone is silent.
Email, cell phone, voice mail: everything silent.

Baba Yaga:

The wind blows the scent of orange across
the garden. Cedar fingers snap. The sea
swishes the shore. Even traffic has melody.

Sadie:

On my wedding day I was so happy. A miracle.
The adventure begins. Two people, harmony,
learning to dance in rhythm. Connection.

Baba Yaga:

All things come together, then separate.
It is the dance.

Sadie:

Statistics say the happiest people are married men
over sixty-five.

Baba Yaga:

And the women?

Sadie:

I will join LavaLife. Chat rooms. Fix
my profile. Send positive protons
out to the universe. Learn to flirt. Buy
a new wardrobe. Thin out.

Baba Yaga:

The heron stands on a deadhead in the river.
She waits, watches, strikes.

Sadie:

Think of all I've learned; second time around,
another chance to do it right.

Baba Yaga:

Weave the colours of the evening sky:
violet and fuchsia,
aquamarine

Sadie:

Three women at a bridge table.
A single woman at a tango club.

Baba Yaga:

The tapestry under my fingers
woven from bone and flesh and thought.

It goes well.

Crazy Jane Resolves the Argument

Body is soul's
borrowed room.

Body needs a mirror,
to see itself.

Soul needs only an empty canvas,
a blank page.

Lead your lover to the bed,
let your long hair cover him.

Then bind your hair in rags,
roll up your sleeves,
select your brushes,
the smooth dip of crimson
on canvas:
let him sleep.

Heron, Daffodil

He is many shapes,
his neck, a long zed,
waiting for fish
or a passing dragonfly;
he is a hunched hobo
huddled in many feathered overcoats.
He is a slow serpentine shadow
across the sky.

Every morning as I drive
across the bridge, he is motionless
on a piece of deadwood in the river,
his world, fish and silence,
mine, noise and words.

He has waited for hours,
a gray silhouette on the still water,
as I pound my horn, grind brakes,
fishing for something
nameless and evanescent
in the red of traffic: the curve
of hillside somewhere else —
a single daffodil sunlit
and swaying in a breeze off the moors
a place elsewhere and forgotten.

Crone

Old crone, you call me, witch woman, hag.
Children run from me, young men
turn their faces. The girls titter like sparrows,
hide behind their hands. They are afraid
of what they do not yet see
in their mirrors — wrinkles etched from smiles
and frowns, skin stretched and hanging
like empty wineskins, or translucent
across veins and tendons.
Bones make scratchy noises
when I walk.

Does this scare you? If you're lucky
you too will wear your skin loosely, will dance
to the music your bones make.
What can we not do, once free
of the shelf-date?

Seeking Baba Yaga

1

She is not kind. The milk she gives
is from the rattler, her touch
like the scorpion's pinch.
There is no softness in her face. She does not need
you or anyone. She scorns gifts
of wedding bands or small infants.
But I have none of these
to give her.

2

"Holy One," I say in my best voice,
"I come to seek your power."

3

"You are just like the others," she says.
"You come with empty hands,
asking me to fill them."

She directs me to a small room. "There
is my power. Weave me a tapestry
and you will learn my secret."

4

There is nothing in the room. The walls
are dun, the floor is dirt — wide as my stretched
arms, high as my lowered head. There are no
windows and the door has disappeared.
What can I weave
out of emptiness?

5

"Start with yourself," the walls whisper.
Tear strips from skirt and jacket,
pluck hair from scalp and eyebrows.
Make a frame from the splintered ceiling —
cobwebs for warp and woof, the bright carapace
left from the spider's latest meal woven
in and out of the coloured strips. Add
an ochre paste blended of dirt
and spit, a drop of blood, mix what you find
in the ground beneath, fingernails in earthen
floors. The ants bring small drops
of water, just enough, but hunger
is part of the tapestry, and thirst.

6

She is not waiting for me, or listening.
I will weave, or the walls
will bury me.

7

My tapestry grows, its reds and blues
bridge light; valleys of green spring
from the shadows. Time eats the walls
of the room as I slide the threads through
skin, through earth, weave the air and the rivers.

8

"Good," says Baba Yaga.
"Now you have begun."

Still a Valley

The motel on the edge of town is empty,
its windows boarded up, the paint dry,
colours fading. Clumps of chicory
edge the roadway, a few blue stalks

still bright in the early sun, and farther on,
wild cyclamen and yarrow line the path
where I walk carefully, the faded map
directing me to cities no longer there.

But the stars are still in their usual places,
the Dipper pours brightness into dim pathways
and though the navigator forgets the names
there still is a valley, a river, a quiet lake

and the old boards will build a small boat
where the water ebbs and flows again.

Boarded Up

I can't write about this,
about mouths open, a tongue worming
against palate, and the noses

where do the noses go?

My mind flounders at buttons,
skin flabby or bumped, what's hiding
behind shirt and belt and trousers —

I can't write about the slow pull
of sleeve from shoulder, a drawing down
of pant from hip, and the underwear

neither silk nor thong nor bikini

That weight in my hand,
the spongy hairiness, the sudden stretch,
the moist bud,

is no longer a thrill down the spine
but a knot in the stomach
a gag in the throat

If it were only fear.
What if it is nothing? How awaken
that heat in the belly, a finger sliding

along the inside of the arm,
lips against the curve of neck,
those places now a boarded up motel

in a town somewhere off the map.

Brief Kiss

That first kiss —
after many months of brotherly
pecks on the cheek — and a pause.
If this were thirty years ago
there would have been another,
arms pulling bodies tighter,
balancing of tall to small,
turn of neck and stretch of tongue,
and there would have been
a look, eyebrows raised:
yes?
and there would have been,
somehow, a way to get
to the bedroom, perhaps
still touching, and there would have been
clothes sliding off shoulders
and belts undone, the click
of buckle, cottons and silk
waterfalling to ankle, step out
and in, bend to the bed, fall
back, stretch and clutch,
eyes leaning toward skin,
the soft places and the hard.

But this kiss is brief —
his armour has slipped
for only a moment, clanks back on.
And after so many years,
how does the body I am in shed
its carapace? Hardened with disuse,
the muscles forget. Even the mind
can only nibble at the edges
of an image: legs and arms
and lips, somewhere. A door opens
and closes.

In the Bird Sanctuary

You show me how to hold my hand still,
palm open, a small mountain of seeds,
and the chickadees come. One small bird
clips from branch to branch, dips down
to my finger; his claws grip, he bends
a yellow beak, takes one seed; then the flutter,
the black head nodding, the swift retreat.

We walk down trails, careful not to tread
the toes of mallards, search for sandhill
cranes, the fledgling eagle in the fir,
the humps of heron in the river,
mute swan hiding under one wing. Friends,
not yet lovers, hovering between
affection and flight.

A Very Tiny Movement in Some Direction

He sends an email, *re: getting together*,
hesitates about our dinner plans.
His fingers are black with the soot
of sad affairs, an empty marriage.
He wants to think, as if thought
was what this was about. Perhaps
he will choose flight, or hibernation,
pace the shores of the lake, listen
to the loon's cry. Perhaps I will be the one
to turn away, though that is not
likely. But after such a long time,
can I feel again, body closed
like a rose in autumn, petals brittle
as old paper, bud hidden in a tight
carapace? Perhaps I should unlock
the door of his cabin, wearing only
my fearful skin, feel my way
across the wooden floor, watching
for the light from whatever window
is open.

Rehearsal

1

How will it be, when he —
when I, if I, if he —
moves from this careful opening,
this basket of cobras, this cave of spiders —
What eyes are needed to perceive
a slow unfolding of wings, petals
of great delicacy, mango on the tongue?

2

We walk to dinner, yards apart, he stops to emphasize a point, it
takes me a few minutes to realize he is not beside me. When we
talk, we look straight ahead, words cool in the autumn air, brush-
ing like hummingbirds with another place to go, no honey here,
nothing to catch the tumbling of the blood, the tippling of the
heart. Or is this the way it is, when the blood slows and the knees
rust and the mind turns each leaf over looking for flaws?

3

In the movies, lovers toss off their clothes
as if they were paper: buttons
burst, zippers slide, silk rips slickly,
and the body beneath is airbrushed, oiled,
long-legged and perfect.

4

Perhaps this is only a rehearsal,
take five, try again, rewrite the script,
stitch another costume, remake the set.
Perhaps this actor is only one of the stunt men
standing in for the real thing, the real thing
still memorizing his lines, bandaging his wounds,
wandering in his own dark desert.

As If

Affairs of the heart will go well this week.
— Libra horoscope, Dec. 27, 2007

As if a horoscope could urge him
into action, not the retreat
you predict. As if
you could walk into his room, pull off
your trenchcoat, step naked
into his bed, coat in a heap
on the floor. As if
you could wipe his chart clean, fix
the angles and squares, reverse
the retrogrades. As if
the planets would realign, the houses
shift, Venus lift her skirts out of Virgo
and ride a Sagittarian centaur into another
chapter, the best one. As if everyone
lives happily ever after, for is this not
a comedy? As if
all tragedies are just unfinished comedies
and the hero doesn't really die, just
waits his turn to figure it all out.

Desire

The hummingbird in the hawthorn
day after day, on the top branch:
his long bill plunders the air
his wings sing the cold away.

The star magnolia unfolds each bud
stretches out of its velour coat
one long finger at a time
testing the wind, its chilly edges.

The daffodil keeps its green hood
dawdles its long neck while the frost
leaves footprints on the window
and the sun sets thin shadows on the lawn.

Not yet. Not yet. The hummingbird
hovers in the air,
the magnolia huddles near the wall,
the daffodil hides its yellow.

Each day, a little more.
The night folds back on itself.
Patience, you say:
the bird on the branch, humming the air.

Nothing between Us

I have woven a parachute
out of everything broken.
— William Stafford

There was nothing between us, really:
some walks through the ravine,
one evening full of stars:
Orion, Draco, Deneb,
Cassiopeia, a day in the bird
sanctuary. We were friends,
chatted over email, told each other
stories. We shared nothing
but words and hours, and
I have woven a parachute

out of that nothing, something
to hold us if we stepped together
off the cliff, some flimsy thoughts
to tie onto our backs, but he wants
nothing. And the fall is long
though the scenery on the way down
is familiar. I know the sting
of the rocks to come, the blood
and bruises, and how to make a home
out of everything broken.

Not This Time

Warm affectionate regards, he writes, working hard
not to say love. Shutting all doors with padlock and bolt,
a troop of guard at the gate. No use
to wave flags or skirts, no point learning tango,
the sensuality of surrender. Not this time
not this man.

The world slides its axis away from the window
where the hawthorn blooms in white and green.
The blackberry scratches its way to my door
offering leaves and small buds, no berries. If I took
a hatchet, I could create a garden
from what I desire, if I knew what I desire.

Let the weeds offer their tangled blossoms:
broom and lupin, wild sweet pea. Let the rose
complain of neglect, and the blue hydrangea
grow leggy and thin, strangled in crabgrass.
Let the lambs-quarters, the cheatgrass,
the thistle and chicory, let the bindweed
glory the fence, the chickweed climb
the rockery. Let this be
my garden.

Exit Scenarios

Josh

He unlocked the front door,
still wearing the cold from the morning,
took off his helmet,
his blonde hair receding at the temples,
balding on top. *I missed the turn
to your place,* he said, *almost made it
to my office instead. That means something.*
She hung up his jacket in the closet,
made tea, ignored his words. Later,
they made love on the yellow sheets,
the driftwood bed. He left her key
by the table.

Jeff

In the restaurant, he leaned
over the plate of steak and salad.
*You let me walk all over you,
treat you like a piece of shit.*
She looked carefully at him —
the long hair, oily, the face
with its grin, the thin shoulders.
She'd come such a long way,
and to hear such words.
She lay down fork
over knife, settled the cape
over her shoulders,
walked out.

           Years later,
they met, sat at another restaurant. *What
did you do?* she asked, *after I left?*

I ate my dinner, he said, *later*
ordered coffee. Admired your perfect
exit, your cape swinging
through the glass doors.

  John
He had already cleared the closet
before she returned from work,
though she didn't know that
till later. He greeted her at the door
glass of scotch in his hand,
poured her one. Together,
on the sofa, they talked —
easy married words, then:
I'm in love with another.
He said he would stay the night —
she thought that was a good sign.

Chagall's Lovers

In the painting by Chagall her eyes of love
upside down, the eyes where mouth should be,
her mouth a pouting *bindu* at her brow
her curling hair, an enigmatic beard.

Her lover leans toward her, smugly,
puts a hand upon a perfect breast —
two small globes; inside, two dots of brush.
His smile a darker echo of her own.

Head over heels in love, she is tuned
to nuances in fingers, hand and eyes.
A fugue in flute and clarinet, the theme:
Eve unclothed and ready, while her mate

clothed and hidden, taking with some glee
each breast of apple fallen from the tree.

The Master's Response

for Patrick

Now that's a bad poem, he'll finally say,
turning to the others. Do you see?
Here the structure forces words to creep,
to crush, to bounce, to squeeze into a line

without intent or meaning. Like this one:
her eyes of love, upside down . . .
Now, eyes of love. We've been through that — *show
don't tell.* Who can see those eyes

and know if love, or fear, or mere desire?
And the meter, those mindless bonks
that plod a thought like lemmings to the cliff:
the Pied Piper of iambs, tuneless trills.

The hard choices of line length — we've been through it.
Look at McKay, at Gilbert: go and do it.

Icarus Diving

He stood at the edge of the cliff,
his body a thin crescent
arching against the wind, lean
and desperate, holding the sun like a mango,

leaning on nothing, and I watched as the
cliff folded itself around him,
a crescent of sky above, his bright
mango-coloured hair shining

and the water, the crescent-shaped pool, the rocks,
their bold angles, the leaning branches of willow,
and the body, falling, the cliff behind him,
and the sun, a green fire, and the blue water.

What to Bring

*after Linda Pastan's
"Almanac of Last Things"*

I choose the hyacinth
for the sharp sweet smell
of its many blossoms
and how swiftly
it turns. And I choose
the sonnet for how it spills
so much into so small a container.
I choose February
because it balances despair
and hope at either end,
and August for its brazen
farewell. I choose
a neat gulp of scotch
to smooth out the awkwardness
of first meeting. and another
to drop clothes and inhibitions
from tight shoulders. From the book
of last things I choose you,
though I don't know your name
or when you will find me.
And I choose twilight
because of the slow settling
from bright to pale to dark
and the stars that finally
appear.

Could

after Susan Stenson's
"Could Love a Man"

I could love a man
whose bald head shines like an apple
whose shape is of a pear
who smokes
marijuana with his grandchildren
so they will think he is cool —
who has no secrets but can keep others'
who suffers fools gladly
especially his own fool self.

I could love a man
who thinks with his hands
builds a bookcase
as a Christmas present —
reads, my feet in his lap,
sits in his garden
knows a hundred birds
by their shape in air
their song.

I could love a man
who plays the saxophone
but longs to learn the harpsichord
can be found in small rivers
large kitchens
makes bouillabaisse for twenty
porridge for two
boasts about the fish he caught
the ones that got away.

Online Dating

I thought it could work so easily:
one email then he would fall in love
and so would I.
Every day I checked the website —
same photos: bald men with odd
smiles and strange stories. Wanting
thin young girls, a good laugh.

I wanted a miracle. Someone
whose shelves were stocked
with my grocery list of needs,
and all I had to do was fill the basket,
pay at the cash register —

all I had. And what did I have?
a smart turn of tongue,
a book of poems, something
to urge one foot in front of the other
on cold mornings. Nothing to grab the eye
at a distance. I needed time

I knew I didn't have. Some faith
that desire radiated its own heat
despite the turbulence of the weather,
the small dot on the map
that one breath makes, ragged
and tremulous.

Lollop

One leg shorter than the other,
he lists like a boat
on an uncomfortable sea:
my stomach roils a little
when I see him.

I turn away, my shoulder a wall
against the force of his eyes, my back
to any charm he might lurch
in my direction. Not for me,
I say. And what could I offer

but my bitter expectations:
a perfect mate, hidden away
somewhere, perhaps exploring
a lost river in the Amazon
or running a bareboat charter
out of Italy. Not here, not now

only this lilting and pitching bald guy
with eyes like a child's, open
even to my stiff shoulders,
my lowered head, the no I throw
to all things spotted, torn, mottled,

all things unkempt, undone, disheveled
and disarrayed. And what might lie beneath?
The hidden textures, the colours
and spices: saffron under sawdust,
the lion heart in a hippo's body.

If You Kissed Me

after Dianne Ackerman's "Beija-Flor"

If you kissed me, I'd give up
weekends and late morning lie-ins,
I'd take up rock climbing with an eighty-pound pack
across my shoulders, I'd bury my words
in a cemetery in Nepal, and dig up
new ones on Madagascar, if you kissed
me I'd sky dive from the space station
and discover new planets on the way down,
if you kissed me, I'd catalogue every one
of the seventy thousand species of beetle
and describe each one in loving detail —
if you kissed me, I'd train birds
to fly backwards and the three-toed sloth
to hang right side up, I'd swim
with a Royal Bengal tiger in the Sundarbans
and offer him oolong tea while drying
his orange coat, if you kissed me
mangoes would grow on pine trees
and harvest in a winter storm, I'd
gather rain into a thousand thimbles
and kayak down the pocked surfaces —
if you kissed me small dogs would follow
your drumbeat in my belly and cats
serenade your percussion motion and
I would serenade the sky with all
five thousand colours of the palette —

if you kissed me.

Adam's Dilemma

There are two Creation stories, and
two Adams. Each is within us.
— Rabbi Harry Brechner

It wasn't enough
to be complete within myself,
male and female created he them:
God's words exactly, and within me
the yin and the yang, domination
and surrender, all the creatures,
within me, *in our image*,
declared Elohim to the angels,
the stars, the plants, the mammals,
the fish, the birds. Everything
a part of me and I of everything.
To have dominion, to be a steward
of the realm, to protect the rabbit
from the eagle's clutch, to bring the bees
to flowers and the sea turtles
to sand, to correct the winds
and sweep the shoreline, to douse
the forest fires, bring water
to the desert.
            Something within me
longed for *other*, a mirror to reflect
all the moods and longings that lie
hidden and contained. Someone
to tell, at the end of a day,
that the sky was saffron along the edges
of the clouds, and the sea trembled
as the moon walked along the waves.

What is beauty when it is not shared?
The lion, walking beside me,
is not interested; the hyena
scratches its belly and the eagle
watches the sky under its wings.
Selah, not a rib, but a wall
that leans in and in, towards the other:
skin to skin, my flesh alive
under her hand. Separation,
then completion.
>   Alone
I could lift my arm, touch
the clouds. I knew what I knew.
The grass, the wind, the willows
bending, the smell of summer
in the sagebrush, and I in the centre
of the garden. All the creatures
within me —

and yet, this yearning:
I watch the swans, their long necks
curved toward each other,
gliding in one rhythm — one and one,
and I, one only. Those named joys:
re'ut, the companionship of equals;
ditzah, the delight of sharing;
the challenge of *chevda*,
coming through the chaos we can make
and unmake so easily; *gilah*,
revealing our deepest selves
to each other; *ahavah*, bodies
connected like heaven and earth,
creation in each moment.
To lie down together,
spiral ourselves down
among the ferns and lilies. To know
and not know; to be a mystery

to each other, yet to hold our souls
trembling, in each other's hands.

But to be all in all! To feel
only a little lower than the angels,
to know the ways of the wolf
and to leap with the ibex
along Ein Gedi's rocky hills:
to sit at the edge of the water
hearing only its trill and trickle —
all creatures
within me, me alone,
the voice of Elohim
at my ear, the stars a halo
around my head:
why is this not enough?

In Everything
That Sings

—

This thou perceiv'st, which makes thy love more strong,
To love that best that thou must leave ere long.

— SHAKESPEARE, SONNET 73

Breath

I wanted to think we were playing some game,
you'll do this thing, this dying, then we'd all get up
play another round of Rummy Q, go to the White Spot,
and you'd order your usual breakfast: pancakes, coffee,
and I'd go back to work, return on the weekend when
we'd do it all again. I never thought you'd take a breath
and then no other, though even that last breath
was followed by one more, and I thought another
would follow, but you lay still, your mouth softened,
your skin slowly turned to a waxy yellow,
not yellow exactly but cream, a peaches and cream
complexion, and you allowed your youngest daughter
to wash you, shave you, dress you
in clean pajamas while I, your eldest daughter,
called your sons and your sister and the rabbi,
called the funeral arrangers, noted the time,
signed the forms, and you lay alone,
somewhere else but only sleeping —
you seemed only to be sleeping, though the pulse
at your neck that I watched all last night —
its steady, comforting beat — was still.

Well, Hello

The morning of his funeral was a bright cold day.
My father lay in his pine coffin
a blue velvet sheet over it,
with Hebrew words written in gold.
I wanted to know where his head was
so that I could lay mine beside his,
wrap myself in his *tallis*:
but he's not here —
he is in the cold wind
when we open the chapel doors.
He is in the yellow crocus at the edge of the cemetery,
in the ripple of water in the stream —
not under his heavy blanket of earth,
the flesh of his head so thin,
his white hair dry as desert grass.

The night before he died I held his hand,
my fingers counting the pulse at his wrist —
I listened to his breathing, ten sharp ones,
then a long slow sigh,
and a ragged breath again:
the body persistent, the spirit
wishing to slide away in that lengthening pause.
"You can let go, Dad," I told him,
obedient to the books and nurses.
"We're all ok. We'll take care of Mom."
But I wanted my father's blue eyes
open again. "Well hello!" he'd say,
walking sprightly to the living room.
"Let's play," he'd say. "Deal me in."

Everything That Sings

His soul is in everything that sings:
winter wren in the hawthorn,
sparrow whose song
is longer than his small body,
moon's round rhythm,
crescendo of hill and valley.

In everything that sings:
pebbles that tune the river,
susurration of tide,
wind circling the autumn leaves
light humming in an Arctic sky
adagio of moonlight on the water.

Still We Know

Loss makes great value
of small things: a spiderweb
in an empty room.

Loss — such a small word,
galaxies of starless nights
felt under the ribs —

makes Doubt a daily
visitor, who laughs
when you talk of filling gaps.

Great idea! he says,
his voice edged in black,
his teeth a mocking white.

Value is what you find
on e-bay, he taunts:
all pennies and dimes

of not much; subtract
beyond zero and nothing
remains. Yet the stars,

small points of brightness
in a dark sky, endlessly
gleam, despite cloud or

things which make the light
invisible. Still we know,
somewhere, or believe,

a tiny light is enough
to keep the demons we create
harnessed.

Spiderwebs catch
the corners of the room, form
lifelines tough as diamonds

in patterns finer
than Belgian lace, and though
a moth, a beetle, or

an errant silverfish
is nowhere near, yet
she spins beauty into

empty space, from her
own tumbling galaxy
which catches each

room's waiting breath,
the pause before the silence
when the stars sing.

What is Mortal

And when the time comes
I don't understand his dying. Wait
for him to return, know only as the brain knows
he will not be at the door when I come to visit.
Such a simple thing, to love what is mortal —
as if there is anything else to do.

The red pepper in the planter
has finally unclutched its hand
from the dead twig, and the maple
spreads small red leaves on the rock.
The hawthorn is bare.

My father's closet
Somewhere a man wears his jacket,
collar lifted against the cold.
Hands in the pockets, what would he find?
An extra pen, a stick
of Wrigley's Juicy Fruit,
three nickels.

Red bathrobe
hangs on the back
of the bathroom door.

Sometimes in the night
my mother puts it on, her arms
in its empty sleeves, imagines
his arms around her

Migration

Where are you? Gone, says my sister.
In the clouds and the wind, says my niece.
With God, says the rabbi.
I dream of the coyote we saw
that day on the city lawn. Is this you?

Soudade

The longing for something that doesn't exist.

Night

The nights are long, my mother
sleeps on her deaf ear, wakes early.

Cleaning up

A tape in a box behind the rusted bike —
my father's voice, all his songs:
"Sunrise, Sunset" at family weddings.
"Yevorechecha" at bar mitzvahs; the song
he sang to my mother
on their 50th wedding anniversary:
Till all the seas run dry,
till then I'll worship you, dear.

What it was like

They were still making love
a month before he died.

Some marriages work, I don't know
how. "Chemistry"
my mother tells me. "Just one look."

I look and look:
nothing happens.

His last days

Early mornings in February:
daffodils push up the ground
with their green spines, snowdrops
like white tears. "Hurry up spring," I say,
wanting my father to see flowers,
feel heat. Instead,
we buy ice cream,
taste summer, our fingers cold.

Who else

will sing like him? And who
will call the wheelchair, *his stroller*,
will say to his wife, when she asks
who they should tell he is dying:

Well honey, you should hire
the plane that will fly a banner
across the sky.

Kaddish

The coffin seems so flat
and I imagine him
wrapped in white,
his tallis around his head

how can he move
to turn over
in sleep? And how

can he see me?

All I Can Think About

My nieces say, oh there's a rainbow
There's *Zayda* in the wind and the water.
There's *Zayda* in the budding of the trees
the cherry blossoms, the robins.
I walk through the labyrinth with my grief,
follow its winding stones. Going forward,
I am turned back. In any direction

all I can think about is my father.

And I can't write about the sun on the cedars
or a hand on my belly in slow morning sleep,
and I can't write about wild geese
their tucked wings in the long grass.
I write about how he walked to the piano,
touched the keys, said, "I can't sing any more,"
but he sang anyway, low, coaxing us:
Yevorechecha. A blessing.

And even then, all I can think of are the last days
his stumbling walk, the swollen feet
my sister and I massaged each night, the bones
of shoulder and arm, so thin.
"All we have is now," he said, "don't hurry,"
and we covered him with blankets,
hoping for spring and a fine morning.

All I can think about is my father.

The way they bundled his body, tied
it with ropes and belts, stood him upright
in the elevator, slid him into a white van.
It's just a body. But *his* body.
I wanted to know where his head lay
in his blue coffin, so that I could talk to him,
hear his voice again, not the voice of the wind
or the sea's measures, not the thunder or the rain
on a still lake, not the surf mumbling on sand
or echoes in a distant valley.

All I can think about
is my father.

His Voice

because my father lived his soul
love is the whole and more than all
— e.e.cummings "my father moved
through dooms of love"

It has been nine months since my father died,
a different kind of birthing,
and only last week, my daughter said,
"I miss him," as if we had been waiting
for his return from wherever he had been
and only now, we understood.
The empty space at the table
remains empty. Now is the time
for remembering.
Because my father lived his soul

in all he did, we can listen to his voice
on the tape he made, his droll
jokes, the way he'd tease
the waitresses, the turn of his tongue
on words — the small words that turned
dark to bright. His song in my head
as I listen carefully. Will he not
return? And will we know him —
in a dream, in a catch of the heart, when
love is the whole and more than all.

My Mother Gives Away
My Father's Clothes

I hope some man
sits on the corner of Douglas and Yates
wearing my father's neatly pressed trousers

I hope he's singing

I hope someone falls in love
with his voice

takes him home with her

folds his trousers carefully on the chair
beside her bed

listens. Listens.

Rainbow Skirt

for my mother

She sits in the bleachers, Keefer Ball Park, 1932,
wearing her rainbow skirt with its tight pleats.
She straightens each fold, patting
the nubby wool, pulling the skirt
neatly over her knees. She leans down,
watching the boy who will become my father
hit his famous home run.

Yesterday, her father had refused
to buy the skirt for her. "You don't need
anything," he told her. "Besides, I'm saving
for your brother to go to college."
She wanted to go to college too, become
an English teacher. The door to his pawn shop
closed behind her, Hastings Street was dark
and cold. In front of her, caught in the sidewalk crack,
a five dollar bill. Just enough.

Now, smoothing her dark blonde curls,
she makes new plans. She will be his bride,
raise his children. Buy a house. Her daughters
will go to college. This will be enough.

Conjuring My Grandmother

for Mary Izen z'l

Why have you called me back,
what have I to offer you?
You know my story —
at least as much as your mother knows:
Father in jail, Mother in a madhouse,
the aunt who took me in as her servant.
I was so glad to be sent to America,
even if it was to another aunt,
a looser kind of bondage.
And then, that man: your grandfather.
The worst prison, blessed by God —
invisible chains, his hands
holding me down. Never let your dreams
be tarnished! Better no dream at all —
better to scrub floors, make bread,
serve meals, than to gaze out the window
to an empty garden.

When he died, I bought a little house,
I could walk to *shul*, curse God
and praise him for each day's rising.
I could take off the rings
which bound my fingers,
comb my graying hair, climb into bed
with only one pillow. Was I happy?
Why do you want to know?
The absence of unhappiness is
good enough.

Lilacs grow in the backyard — they were there
when I arrived. The maple tree
offers green and then yellow and red.
The little seed cakes your mother brings
taste delicious. Do I regret, you ask:
do I wish for something more? Drink your tea.
Have a little seedcake. Don't
look out the window.

Instructions for Dreaming

Approach the dream like a lover,
scrubbed and empty, hands open:

lie down with blessings, pray
for light, a good dream,

one that wakes you in the night
with a clear voice, your own,

not one that leads you down a path
you have already been on and learned nothing.

Are you ready? Have you bathed in cool water, brushed
the day from you, dressed in clean robes?

—

Have you learned the stillness
at the centre of things,

slow spiral of body to the heart's core;
time blurs as the music rises

in the throat of the sparrow
in the branches of the willow, water

at the sand's edge — your father's tenor
soaring above the choir: *hashkivenu*

twilight through the stained glass windows
light like a benediction, a hand on your head.

—

Will the dead return, in dreams? Disguised
as a river, a coyote with mangled fur,

an empty hillside, an attic room in a forgotten
mansion, a bird with bent wing? Or as himself

wrapped in a comforter, offering lifesavers
and good advice. Descend the stairs

into a stone cavern, butterfly like lace
shadowed on the walls.

Watch the wings emerge and flutter,
blood through veins, a river of red.

—

Every night I lie down and ask
the impossible: come back

in your own skin, the moles on your neck
your crazy teeth, your white hair —

sleep beside my mother and tell her
everything you know. Remind me

how your eyes saw everything good
and where I can find you. Show me

what there is to do yet, and how
to live in this broken world.

Directions of the Heart

—

*Why do you dress me
in borrowed robes?*

— SHAKESPEARE, *MACBETH*, I. III

Taking Apart a Solid Sense of Self

It helps that you live in a human body,
one that will inevitably
fall apart anyway and no steel
will hold it together. Swiftly
or slowly, all its parts that once flourished —
bone and muscle and heart and brain —
will flounder. Perhaps it will be the joints first,
those intricate ball bearings of shoulder,
angle of elbow, the swivel of hips
that will rust in place, un-oiled,
or tatter at the boney edges. Or perhaps
it will be the skin, loosening
like old fabric, or drying out
like cracks in a desert landscape.
More likely it will be those invisible parts
that churn and rustle,
that pound and push, that jump
across cells and synapses, those parts
that open and close. And who are you
if not those cells, those wasted atoms
you have ignored so long. What self
can walk away, shed the skin, unhinge
the knees and hips, blow the last breath
into a place somewhere else, or not at all?

Four Directions of the Heart

with a line borrowed from Patrick Lane

1

The English oak outside my window:
paper brown leaves, though it is winter,
brittle, cramped at the edges.
If they were bone they would be broken
if they were glass they would be shattered —
they clutch the throat of the branches:
until there is a bud of new green
they won't believe.

2

Her smile. It *has entered him*
like a cage enters an animal. No matter the smile
leans in another direction. Like a weather vane
it blows eastward and westward, and he stands
northerly. He counts the teeth of her smile
in each bite, chews the crumbs.
He loves the shining bars
in front of his eyes, the cold shadows.

3

By the doorstep, honeysuckle
in small clay pots, cracked with growing.
Sun and a bit of earth is all
it needs. Yellow shadow inside white,
its scent on the wind, like the sound of a flute
meandering down the alleyway.

4

Proud flesh, it's called: that ridge of skin
that shapes a scar. Stronger than before the flesh
tore, the knife slashed a red river in a hill of skin:
the cliff, the fall, the pieces held together
by mere stubbornness. Stronger
than anything.

Six Months

for my daughter

Maybe it's your toes I like best
the small pea shape, their roundness

in my mouth, your chortle
as I slide my tongue around each one.

Or is it your ear, its meandering
curves, the little hole I blow into.

Or the fuzz of your hair, duck down,
commas of curl at your neck.

Or maybe your hand, as it strokes
my breast, and we are two curves

of arm and back and maybe what I love
is the blue of your eyes, the way they see

the world as all yes —
and the way you wake in the morning

smelling of piss, drenched and laughing.

Walk On

a fugue

The first time she stood, her own feet
holding her, balance of knee and thigh,
eyes forward, her diaper sliding
perilously down, barefoot,
wearing a shirt I had embroidered in the days
she would lie still in a crib —
the first time she knew she didn't need me
to taxi her across the room,
eyes forward to where she wanted to go —
the embroidered days of breast
and sleep gone now: she balanced
need in her perilous glance, here
and here, no longer still in a crib
but standing, her own feet
marking the path embroidered
with perilous ledges, a highway
across winter, always forward
in her balance of need and knowing,
and I taxi her around
in my mind, embroider her days
with my perilous love:
cribbed and almost silent.

Magnolia

Beside the window, a star magnolia, bare
branches, a few stubborn leaves
once green, now edged with brown —

tips of the branches like down,
like your head under my hands
blonde fuzz. Wide-eyed baby, eyes

that looked upon the new light
like a conqueror, just landed
on a blue shore. So long ago.

Now, we talk, we are careful to show
only the safe side of our hidden worlds.
"Don't tell me that," you warn, a fence

of silence, of things too tense
to mention, even in a poem. The old leaves
stiffen against the wind, rain

softens its fist, but for now, restraint
is our only growth, one small white star
at a time.

Mothers, Daughters

An anvil upon which to forge
identity. Sparks. Fire. Danger.

The strongest of bonds. The cord cut,
like a lost limb, always tugging.

A rocking chair. A long night. Listening
for breath, in, out. Finally the dawn.

How can something inside you
be outside? How to let go?

This is me. This is not me.
Bones, cells, muscles, mind.

Unravelling, strand by careful strand.
This takes time. The wind through the body.

What to hold? What to let go?
Even untangled, torn, even gone — a ghost.

Telenagging, she called it.
The mother in the mind.

Distance makes no difference. Only
for rescue. There is no rescue.

There is no retreat. The invisible cords,
a kind of music. Learn to listen

and not listen. Shut off the noise,
hear the melody of the bones

what rivers we remember
what valleys, the women we are.

On the Doorstep

On my thirtieth birthday, I thought I was
pregnant, imagined walking along a shore
holding the hand of a small child.
I had quit my job a few months before,
moved out of my apartment,
moved in with a friend. Last week
I had rear-ended my lover's car, following
too close. It was over anyhow.
And there was no child. No job. No house.
But the sun shone, the water shimmered
black and white-capped;
snow already on the distant mountains.

I've been told all prayers are answered, but
the time between prayer and answer may be long
and we turn to the lesser dream, impatient,
while our prayer sits on the doorstep, door
closed and no one home. How long the wait:
for the call, the letter, the trek
through the desert to end —
how long the distance seems
from one green garden to another.
Patience is a clock we hold in our hand,
demanding its ticking fit our own
heart's percussions, afraid to wait
for the slow pendulum to return —
as it has. As it will.

Classroom

The boy with the cap turned backwards
sits close to the door for escape;
the recent couples, fingers locked, no room for pencils
or anyone else;
the one with drifting eyes chooses the window
where one leaf falls
slowly from the maple
and the grass grows green from term to term.
In small clumps of talk or silence
they've entered the classroom, chosen
their encampments.

One or two sit directly in front; they
will have good marks and no friends.

A group of six or seven, whose young and restless
lives will run in parallel, in gossip
or flirtation the rest of the semester —
they've set up their camp
miles and miles from the front of the room
where a still figure watches.

The bell rings and a Pavlovian dimming
of talk and movement; a few
will slide off jackets, pull back
hoodies, but most prefer their suits
of hibernation, the long winter
of adolescence. Except the girls —
their sky-blue bra straps on curved
shoulders, spandex t-shirts
pulled down barely
over breasts, over concave slope
of belly, teasing cliff of hipbone —
winter and summer in one hot room.

Like animals on either side of the water-hole
sniffing for danger.

What Does She Want from Us?

She says to write a sonnet — just like that!
As if to sit and write is simple stuff,
blend thought to feeling, add a little fluff
of metaphor perhaps: in seconds flat!

She thinks that we can finish every task
that she assigns us, that we have no other
work to do, or time to spare, or any mother
down our backs, that we can simply bask

on our porches, pen in hand, the sounds
of gentle music in the background — sure,
in your dreams! whatever! there's no cure
for work and work and deadlines, and the frowns

of teachers, parents, adults, everyone
who tells us what to do and how to run.

High School Subtext

They arrive with their own chapters:

    last night Sean's mother threw a shoe
    at his father who threw
    his fist into her cheekbone

    yesterday Carrie's best friend o.d.'d
    on crystal meth, is hanging on
    by a tube in her arm, 24-hour watch

    this morning Jo walked three miles to school,
    holes in her runners collecting small stones,
    her pockets empty, bus fare
    coming in next week's paycheck

    last week Justin tried out
    for the soccer team, but his shoes
    had been stolen, his shorts ripped off
    his thin legs. *Take ballet lessons*
    the others jeered.

    all week Mei Lin from Macao, her first time
    away from home, waited
    for a letter from her parents. These long days
    her few English words insufficient
    for friendship.

They sit at cramped desks, pound
their knapsacks on the floor, glare
around the room, fists reluctant
to hold pencils. I smile gently —
so small a poultice —
read poems that speak words
they don't want to hear:

They have enough of death
and betrayal, know more
than their tongues can slide around a syllable:
Stuff it in a bag, they say
Read us something pretty.

Retirement

At first I thought it would be like death:
someone else's coat over my chair,
my photo gone from the staff chart,
the posters removed, the walls empty
of poems and quotations,
my keys turned in,
my files turned out.
Obliteration: a wiping away, like the words
on my whiteboard, like sand castles
built upon water. Soon there would be no students
who remember me, who tell stories
about that old English teacher:
her wide gestures, her perch
on the ledge in front of the room,
her gargantuan vocabulary, her voice
in their head as she read to them:
To Kill a Mockingbird,
Life of Pi, chapter by beautiful chapter.
As the months moved closer
I began to make lists:
put post-its on every surface,
gathered brochures and college calendars.
Others asked about my plans:
where will you be on the first day
of another year? Will you travel?
Start another career? Become a gardener?
I tell them, I want to learn.

Tom, one of my students,
broke his shoulder and ended his dreams
of Olympic wrestling medals,
like his brothers before him.
Yet he plunges into my room,
eager to tell me about Plato's Cave,
Jung's theory of archetypes, the discoveries
of the Mayans. Did you know,
he says, they predicted changes right into 2012?
I never knew, he says, his eyes alight,
there was so much
to learn.
Who else to become? Musician, singer,
sculptor, writer, full-time poet. Rider of bikes,
walker of shorelines, watcher of birds,
keeper of the garry oak, pruner of thyme and oregano
gone wild, tender of roses and hyacinth.

I count down the days, one by one,
sift through my files, contemplate
a small study shelved with books,
overlooking a garden, under an open window.

School's Out

Fifteen weeks, less three days —
but I'm not counting, no,
nor thinking of what to do
in September, when bells ring
kids and teachers back to school —
back to where I won't be.

I won't be
in the large room near the office, where the days
slow by or swiftly, and the school
books pile on desks or under chairs. No-
where near the basketball rings
or the soccer field — though what I'll be doing

I don't know yet. But what a to-do
I'll make of my leaving! Then, like a bee
gathering summer in rings
of honeycomb, those long days
I'll watch from the patio, and no
one to disturb me, no papers from school

kids, marked and messy. No longer schooled
in the discipline of early morning doings —
shower and dress and maybe eat, or not.
Soon, a slow morning where being
replaces doing. Count each day
by the miles walked, tracing rings

around a field — or by the ringing
of the wood chimes outside the window. And school
fades into old habits, as I make my day
into shapes and patterns, like a new hairdo
or a recycled sweater. Let be,
let be. Make a knot

and tie off those days. Not
grief or regret, but a bright ring
of deeds done — let there be
light, and there is light. School
closes its doors, and I will redo
my life, one languorous day

after the other, the days like small bells
of lily scenting the air, lightness of being, a knot
of joy in the heart's thrum. School's out.

Almost There

Evening. The light
a glimpse through the trees

cold at the edges. Tight
daffodil heads still green.

Slow waking from warm covers.
No. Not yet. Dreams slide away.

Will I waste the years ahead in dreaming?
Lazy on the couch, time clocks by.

Singing lessons. Dance classes. Violin,
piano, tai chi, yoga. Too many plans.

For now, the grass greens
and the light stays like an unexpected lover

one who, years and years later, finds you
sitting at the doorway, looking out.

Undoing

I had forgotten such innocence exists
forgotten how it feels
to live with neither calendar nor clocks.
I had forgotten how to un-me myself.
                          — P.K. Page, "Inebriate"

When I retire, I might write every day
for three hours — a part-time job:
sit at my desk and look out the window,
pen in hand, mind sliding
and holding and letting go.
I will learn something new, some twist
of detail, how the maple seed flies,
the curve of a parabola, the words
of a song or favourite poem — a "being" list:
I had forgotten such innocence exists.

A day to shape to my liking
whatever the outer weather — rain or snow,
winds from the north or the calming south —
let the inner weather be sun,
something to melt the core of fear
or disappointment, yellow dawn that steals
across morning cloud — and the rain
soft at the edge of shore,
summer rain, and the wind at my heels:
I have *forgotten how it feels*

to walk without purpose —
not counting steps or swinging arms
to get all muscles working: exercise
that keeps the body moving on its pendulum:
work, sleep, eat — and then again
and over again, each day, don't stop
to think about it. What's it for?
To watch the eagle watching from the snag,
note the anemone colouring the rocks,
to live with neither calendar nor clocks

I'll throw away the daily planner,
find the centre of a life well-lived
already, moment by simple moment.
Not to be anything but what I am now,
sit and let the blood move me where it will,
let the masks I've worn cobweb on a shelf:
be an empty vessel, let the breath blow
through me, *ruach*, spirit wind that comes
with the tide, sound of the sea and smell of kelp:
I had forgotten how to un-me myself.

Nothing To Be Owned

Only three things:
the hoarse cry of a crow,
a violet crushed,
and you, on the stairs.
— Dorothy Livesay, "Only Three Things"

I pack up my room,
choose which books to take home,
which poems on the wall to frame,
which drawings that I have treasured
all these years — kids
and the colours they fling
onto paper. Give away
the lessons I have made
to others. Bring
only three things.

It's a long walk down the halls,
where lockers clank empty
and the noise of a thousand voices
is finally stilled. Summer —
a pause and an oasis for them,
and the first steps to the place I will go:
a boundless desert of unknowns
where light repairs the shadow in sand,
and the hard sirocco winds blow,
and beyond, *the hoarse cry of a crow.*

There will be beauty, of course —
cleanse the windshield of my eyes
to see the geometry of dunes,
the little cactus at my feet,
the swift lurch of lizard,
the Joshua tree, the thorns of acacia bush.
Everything as it is, infinite —
though I know how swiftly
the hot winds grit and gust,
and the violet, crushed.

Nothing to be owned or taken,
nothing to be earned, by right
or wrong, nothing to be stored away.
What's to come? The clock ticks
in harmony with the stars,
the manna from heaven falls, I wear
my skin lightly, my hands open
for the rain to fall, the long climb up
the bare slopes, the burning sun, the glare —
and perhaps, *you on the stairs.*

Counterpoint and Pause

A kind of paradise. Everything itself.
The sea is water. Stones are made of rock.
The sun goes up and goes down. A success
without any enhancement whatsoever.
　　　　　— Jack Gilbert, "The Other Perfection"

Morning, grey sky and a hint of rain:
the trees a shadow against the eye —
the oak's brown leaves like a mockery
of spring, a brittle offering. Somewhere
behind the clouds, the Olympic mountains
gather snow, the sea calm and cold.
Light a fire and cave yourself in a book,
watch the birds disappear, except for one
that sits patiently at the top of the hawthorn.
A kind of paradise. Everything itself.

The table collects debris: a radio,
a game of solitaire, papers to read,
the hibiscus, its blossoms resting.
The daybook lies empty, the days stretch
into eyes and hands. The heart beats
in irregular rhythms of stress
and patience, a game of waiting —
walk along the beach, collect summer
in crab shells and broken glass:
the sea is water. The stones are made of rock.

The driftwood logs are wood and water. Rocks
climb the cliffs, where broom clutches
the dead tangles of blackberry,
each planning the next invasion.
One white herring gull against the sky,
its call crisps the air, echoes. Everything
waits, a long held breath
as the earth turns away, a scorned lover.
Mornings are cold, the night is chill,
the sun goes up and goes down. A success

if you want to call it that. A reminder: seven
lean years, seven fat ones. Diastole
and systole. The heart pumps and rests,
listening to its own music. You count,
and fear. While the notes lift
and soar, counterpoint and pause,
a fugue of lovely repetitions:
wind and water, the shriek of owl,
the simple song of spring's robin
without any enhancement whatsoever.

Simka

Weather abroad
and weather in the heart come on
regardless of predictions.
— Adrienne Rich, "Storm Warnings"

The Kabbalists call it *simka*, joy
that comes like a small child in the early morning,
leaping onto the bed.
The stories I collect to heat the heart:
one winter, a mushroom that tore
through the asphalt in the driveway;
a man who walked out of an avalanche
with a broken arm; the cancer gone
from my father's brain; two lovers who met
on a computer screen, lasted beyond
the nocturnal linkings of the flesh.

You do not get there by trying. Nor
by flagellations of the body or the mind.
You do not get there by the path
along the highway or through the woods,
though one is better than the other.
Like a labyrinth, it folds upon itself
and you do not know where you are
until you are there, and even then
only time seems to have moved.
But the air is somehow different,
a scent of sea, or a flower
you can't name but remember
from another time. And the bare spine
of a salmon lying on the sand
bends like a peacock feather
and shines in the thin
winter sun.

ABOUT THE AUTHOR

—

Barbara Pelman was born in Vancouver and has lived in various communities in British Columbia as well as in Toronto and London, England. She now resides in Victoria where she has taught high school English for many years. She received her B.A. from the University of British Columbia and her M.A. in English Literature from the University of Toronto. She is an active participant in the Victoria writing community: as a member of the Random Acts of Poetry team for three years; as a featured speaker at Planet Earth Poetry (previously Mocambo Café); and as the instigator, along with her students, of the "Poetry Walls" — poems painted on the hoardings in Victoria's downtown core. Many of her poems have appeared in literary journals, including *Event, Descant, Fiddlehead, The Antigonish Review, The Dalhousie Review, Quills,* and *Contemporary Verse 2.* She has also produced four chapbooks of her poems through her company, Quay Words Press. For the past four years, as the co-ordinator of the "Calling All Artists" project of Congregation Emanu-El, she has helped gather artists of various media to discuss mystical religious texts with Rabbi Harry Brechner and to show their interpretations at a gallery exhibit and in a chapbook. Her first book of poetry, *One Stone,* was published by Ekstasis Editions in 2005.